BEIRUT
BEREFT

BEIRUT
BEREFT

ARCHITECTURE OF THE FORSAKEN
AND MAP OF THE DERELICT

PHOTOGRAPHS BY ZIAD ANTAR
TEXT BY RASHA SALTI

SHARJAH ART FOUNDATION

BEIRUT BEREFT:
ARCHITECTURE OF THE FORSAKEN
AND MAP OF THE DERELICT

Authors: Ziad Antar (Photographs),
Rasha Salti (Text)
Coordinators: Shannon Ayers Holden,
Ahmad Makia, Wasan Yousif
Copyeditors: Eti Bonn-Muller (English),
Ismail Al Rifai (Arabic)
Design: Kemistry Design
Consultants: Karen Marta,
Todd Bradway (KMEC)

This publication first released in 2009
by Sharjah Biennial

Reprinted with minor revisions in
2021 by Department of Learning and
Research, Sharjah Art Foundation

Distributed through partnership with
KMEC Books via:

D.A.P./Distributed Art Publishers, Inc.
75 Broad Street, Suite 630
USA - New York, NY 10004
orders@dapinc.com

For distribution, retail and orders in the
Middle East and MENASA region:

Sharjah Art Foundation
Al Shuwaiheen, Arts Area
PO Box 19989, Sharjah
United Arab Emirates
publications@sharjahart.org
sharjahart.org

English cover image: Cote d'Azur Hotel,
Jnah, built in 1973
Arabic cover image: Murr Tower, Wadi
Abu Jmil, built in 1973

ISBN number 978-9948-02-483-5

Printed in the United Arab Emirates

PREFACE

This book is a new edition of Ziad Antar and Rasha Salti's collaboration *Beirut Bereft: Architecture of the Forsaken and Map of the Derelict*, first produced, exhibited, and published for Sharjah Biennial 9 in 2009. Beirut Bereft began with a 2006 encounter between Antar and Salti, when they discovered that they both had been exploring abandoned, functionless buildings in Lebanon scarred by the traces of war and signs of a failing state. Composed of text by Salti and photography by Antar, the project reveals the relationship between social and physical architecture in postwar Lebanon.

Sharjah Biennial 9, invited artists to utilize the biennial platform for experimentation. The project was also the recipient of Sharjah Art Foundation's inaugural Production Programme, an initiative that aims to be a leading supporter of artists' work. The publication of this new edition by Sharjah Art Foundation of *Beirut Bereft* stems from the Foundation's mission to propagate art from the region and beyond while serving as a vehiclefor the realisation of artists' projects.

10

Current page: Fakhoury Building, Caracas, built in 1984
Facing page: The Germans' Building, Jnah, built in 1980
Previous page: Hotel Versailles, Khaldeh, built in 1973

الصفحة الحالية: بناية الفاخوري، كاراكاس، بنيت عام 1984
الصفحة المقابلة: بناية الألمان، جناح، بنيت عام 1980
الصفحة التالية: فندق فرساي، خلدة، بني عام 1973

BEIRUT BEREFT
ARCHITECTURE OF THE FORSAKEN
AND MAP OF THE DERELICT

PHOTOGRAPHS BY ZIAD ANTAR
TEXT BY RASHA SALTI

[...] I had stopped at the hot, noisy Carrefour de l'Odéon in Paris. The coming and going at the crossroads renders one invisible. One can remain quite still. Keep one's gaze focused in the misty distance, on that past of ours, stranger than death. No one will pay any attention. One can even murmur softly, as I do now: "You know, we shall always be those pioneers with our red scarves. For us the sun will always have that faint tang of brass and the sky the resonance of drum rolls. You can't be cured of it. You can't get over that bright horizon only a few days' march away. What's the point of lying to ourselves? We shall never be like the others, like normal people. For example, like that man I see getting into an expensive car. He glides up to the steering wheel with all the smoothness of a bank card being swallowed by an ATM machine.

The well-upholstered interior simply swallows him. First an arm, tossing his suit coat onto the seat, then a leg, then his head, and –zip!– neat as you please, he slips into it, as if into the soft embrace of a mistress. Smiling, relaxed. With one hand on the wheel, holding a slim, brown cigar, the other keying in a telephone number from memory...

"We'll imitate them. We'll ape their coolness. We'll allow well-upholstered seats to swallow us with the same easy smiles. But when all is said and done we'll always remain those young barbarians we once were, blinded by our faith in that near horizon. One vital element will always be missing when we ape them: knowing how to enjoy it. That's what will give us away..."

–From *Confessions of a Fallen Standard-Bearer* by Andreï Makine

I must have been eleven or twelve years old when I attended my first wake. I grew up in (west) Beirut, during the civil war, death was not uncommon to our quotidian. My mother did not endorse the all-black dress code, she preferred black-and-white or all-grey attire. My recollection of that first wake has faded, I just remember accompanying her and experiencing that social ritual first-hand. I remember that after attending a few wakes, the ritual became commonplace in our social life. In Lebanon, rituals surrounding death are more vested in wakes than funerals. Wakes follow burials, the deceased's body is never displayed to those who come to deliver condolences and to assuage the bereaved in their grief. In spite of newspaper headlines tabulating deaths almost every day as currency of civil war, and in spite of wakes becoming habitual, I never quite grasped the full significance of death.

One of my closest friends at school lost her father when we were fourteen or fifteen years old. He died of complications after a difficult surgery. He was not literally a victim of the civil war. He did not die in the battlefield (so to speak), nor was he the unsuspecting victim of a bullet or shell. He had been a high-ranking officer in the Internal Security forces, his soldierly gait overwhelmed the gentleness of his character, and I had always regarded him with a slightly fearful reverence. A week or so after the wake, I was riding the school bus in the morning, traffic was congested, and I was gazing at passers-by walking hurriedly to work when I saw him! He was right there in front of my eyes, dressed shabbily in patched-up second-hand clothes, selling newspapers and cigarettes. He was real, as real as all the other pedestrians beside him. He was not a ghost, he handed papers through open windows of cars temporarily idling, drivers grabbed the papers and paid him. I was convinced it was him. Maybe he did not die, I remember telling myself, maybe he had simply left the life he led until his supposed death and simply wanted another life. Maybe he was weary, miserable and wanted nothing, nothing, anymore to do with his wife, daughters, son, the nice apartment, the colonel's uniform. Maybe he schemed and feigned a death, to escape that life, maybe that was the only stratagem he imagined to slip away without causing too much of a stir. Death was the currency of war, it's what happened to a lot of people every day. Everything else – divorce, family breakdowns, separations – was unsettling, unnatural tragedy. To my own surprise, I found myself accepting without much hesitation the scenario I had just heaped on the man. I even empathised with his grief, I could almost sense his profound unhappiness with the life to which I imagined he had been captive. I tacitly approved of his choice for a new life. The man had staged his own death, and now he had a fresh start, amongst the society of others, amongst people who struggle to get by every day, selling newspapers, chewing gum, Kleenex or whatever, people who have to walk for an hour or two from where they sleep to where they work, who take the public bus. It was simply what he decided would make him happy, I thought. And that thought filled me with a strange relief.

From that moment, I kept seeing people who I knew had passed away, reappear in entirely different realms of life. Death was no longer the end of life, it was merely the end of a specific kind of living and the conscious shift to another. I knew well how one could be driven to exhaustion, to gasp for breath, to reach the edge of despair. They were familiar to me. So were abrupt and seemingly irreversible departures. Overnight, people packed their bags and left their neighbourhood, their city, their country, for good. In addition to attending wakes, I became accustomed to bidding farewell. Departures seemed irrevocably irreversible, 'goodbyes' and 'so longs', terminal. With postal service entirely defunct and phone lines operational on a whim, there was no hope of maintaining contact. Farewells were more painful than wakes. I – we, those left behind – was being abandoned by those who chose to leave. The blinding pain of enduring (and accepting) being abandoned was only assuaged by the passage of time. Just as with mourning death. Soon enough farewell parties and wakes became confused. I remember being scared of being left amongst those left behind.

I am no longer sure how the war ended. There is a chronology, several actually. And archives, the paper trail of diplomatic negotiations, treaties. Chroniclers will no doubt propose several versions for the ending. There were a few battles that were deemed decisive, if not conclusive, followed by negotiations – kept secret in a remote town in Saudi Arabia – an agreement to end the war, hurried parliamentary sessions, a new president, a new cabinet. Then there were violent protests, tires burned in the streets, the national currency spiraling down to oblivion and the tragic assassination of the new president. All this in the span of one year, even less. A false start, perhaps, but such dramaturgical twists and turns were not uncommon to the narrative of the civil war.

Conspiracy? Always a potent answer in Lebanon. Remarkably, the second attempt at a fresh start was not however befuddled by the outbreak of another round of violence. The fire seemed to extinguish from asphyxiation. So we had ourselves another new president, another cabinet and hurried parliamentary elections. In this second round, the national currency was rescued and stabilised almost suddenly. Some deem this was the marker for the end of the war, reclaiming a stealth control over the national economy. The more conventional parameter, which considers the state's monopoly over the administration of violence, could not have applied because it was handed over to the regime next door, in Syria. Also, some 12 percent of the territory, the southern tip defined by Israel as the 'security buffer zone', was under their occupation. Military resistance remained active there until the Israeli state pulled out its army and dismantled its outposts and local proxy apparatus of control in the year 2000.

There was no date ascribed to the end of the war, nothing we celebrate every year or for which we have anthems. I, for myself, just can't determine the instance when we shifted from living in a state of war to a state of non-war. It was a process, and doubtless it was gradual. But there must have been a morning, one defining morning that marked the first day of the first chapter of the post-war. All fictions have a first chapter, a moment to fasten the arc of their dramaturgy. Maybe the morning is just a detail, the point is that we changed, as if we were impelled and compelled at once. We put on new roles. The victims of the war became the citizens of the recovering, improved, republic, the innocent bystanders became the citizens of the republic, so too became the fighters, militias, heroes and anti-heroes. We were all born anew, citizens of this post-war republic. The warlords became members of parliament and ministers in the cabinet. We voted for them, once, twice, even thrice around. Twenty years on, and they are still in power. Those who were assassinated were replaced by their sons and daughters. Communities and the social network of sectarianism, the fabric of fear and loathing, became the republic's civil society. The transformation was overwhelming, it included people, neighbourhoods, streets and buildings. Those who had left for good returned to visit in the summer occasionally.

Those who died, vanished. My fear of abandon transformed to bereavement. I experienced the full meaning of death, in the post-war, for the first time. The cruel chill of the irreversible end of death. The inconsolable longing for what will never be again. The guidelines for the conversion for us, everyday folk, were at best, vague. The political agreement that defined how the war ended, detailing rules for the republic's transition to peace, and the constitutional safeguards to prevent another war from erupting, were very explicit. Grafted by writ on to the republic's constitution, they preserved the national covenant (the diseased marrow of this state, so to speak) untouched. A decade and a half later, and their wisdom has yet to be fully implemented. For lack of a vision of what the recovering republic was supposed to be, the default cue was an uncritical return to where the country had been before the war started. A pre-war idyllic moment was constructed and we were all ushered to fly back there, only in fast-forward motion to the present. In other words, there was no plan, there was a public relations bonanza to raise monies to rebuild the country, mostly Beirut. Some intellectuals protested in newspapers that the government was keener to rehabilitate stones than people, and 'stones before people' became an adage. Taxi drivers, shopkeepers, ambitious politicians and activists recanted it, tirelessly.

Over the seventeen long years, traces of shells, bullets, fire and sniping had spared only a few buildings. Besides basic public amenities, such as highways (a euphemism for roads with several lanes), bridges, thoroughfares, underpasses and overpasses, the airport, seaport and a few other such landmarks, the government had no intention to undertake or participate in the repair of anything else. Not a stone. The scheme was to instigate a momentum by underwriting a plan for the rehabilitation and reconstruction of the city's old pre-war centre, Beirut's downtown. A private real-estate company, exempt from taxes and scrutiny and impervious to public debate, was mandated to overhaul the infrastructure of Beirut's charred and ravaged downtown and to lease it, in turn, to other private developers to transform anew.

I remember distinctly when I first noticed a traditional building get patched up and repainted. It was located on an intersection of what was known during the war as the 'green line', or the snaky thoroughfare that had divided the city into two bellicose halves. The repainting was neither deft nor spiffy, there was nonetheless something remarkable about it, like a proud herald of doing right. We had grown accustomed to the sight of maimed facades and collapsed buildings, walls and roofs agape. It did not seem so crucial to hurry up and fix whatever could be fixed, these markers of destruction – and hurt – had stopped being sore to the eyes. They were our lot, they cohered with everything else with which the civil war had left us. They propounded their own 'genre aesthetic'. Much ink was spilled on their being 'modern ruins' or 'ruins of modernity', and much bromide diluted to capture their poetry, or some other deeper meaning locked within.

Temerarious tourists in the early years of the post-war would get all hot and bothered by photographing and documenting the remains of the buildings. As we guided them, we told stories about everyday survival – for entertainment and, no doubt, to unburden ourselves from the dead weight of grief. The other sightseeing the country had to offer was of ancient ruins, the kind that Mediterranean cities with a fetching history claim as far back as the Roman and Phoenician eras. Those ruins, all archaeological, were in contrast to the modern remains, evidence of past glories, not tragedies. Glory does not make for a fertile field to extract or inspire metaphor and allegory, except for virile nationalism off course, but that's a whole other story. The ruins of our war, reeking of modernity and its disenchanting thereafter, were by far more potent signifiers. Some deemed them monuments, totemic reminders of what we had done to ourselves and to this country, and some, of what others had done unto us. It was argued that at least a few had to be conserved in their state of devastation to prevent the people of Lebanon, and those who malign their senses, from surrendering to the demons of belligerence. In 1992, the republic was nearly fifty years old; it had endured three conflicts in the vein of civil war (two near misses and a really long one), the notion that internecine fighting was endemic to its destiny gained notable currency in the post-war. It resurrected a spectre of doom and cast it in the horizon, far, invisible yet tangible, sometimes drawing ominously nearer and suddenly, by felicitous intervention from Higher powers, pushed to safe distance again.

The momentum of reconstruction and rehabilitation was seriously boosted after the government's spin and public relations machine was cranked up. Facades were spackled; double-bolted metal doors, supplementing safety to wooden doors, were either removed or left wide open, idle, pointless. Keys to their locks thrown to the bottom of a drawer, forgotten for lack of use. Shops began to leave their glass windows exposed at night, the heavy metal shutters that protected them from stray bullets after dark were no longer pulled down. The lights were kept on. Commercial thoroughfares became less lugubrious and daunting at night, they even made for a pleasant promenade. The worn-out, glib discolouring of buildings was revived with a fresh coat of pastel paint. Beirut's languorous, luminous Mediterranean palette slowly found its way back. Feasting on long meals, set in places at a carelessly long drive away, which lasted until right before sunset or sunrise, was back. Frivolous, uncanny cravings and their pursuit were back. Riding through the complicated geography of the diminutive country felt like gliding into an open horizon. The prohibitive impact of checkpoints waned, in spite of their persisting presence. Phones were working again, so was reconnecting with estranged friends, exchanging numbers with new acquaintances, cancelling appointments on the spur, booking theatre tickets, calling lovers at untoward hours and hunting down adulterous spouses...

Some of us, born right before or during the war, did not even suspect we would live any such things, we were novices at the joie de vivre once earmarked as Lebanon's raison d'être. The wild nights were back. They had not stopped during the war, quite the contrary, but they were wholly different then. Back then, they were fuelled by a fierce drive to counter the ravages of violence, and were thus tainted with surrealism and dementia. 'Rage against the dying of the light' took an unwittingly moonstruck twist then. The wild nights of the post-war had none of that stomp, they were like the contrived and rehearsed, uninhibited night play that every city captive to class contradictions and underdevelopment imagines as cosmopolitan jet-setting in this unipolar age of extremes. Between its self-constructed mythology as the Arab capital for perdition and glamour and the compulsion to improvise 'a good living' in times of non-war, Beirut became, giddily, the indulgent holidaying destination for Arabs with means and predilection for sins of the flesh.

Often awake before dawn, I lay in bed listening to the silence, waiting for the sound of bullets and shells to explode in the far-off distance. Nothing. Instead, were occasional cars screeching from unrestrained speed, and primal screams of drunken homebound partygoers. And rubbish collectors, the most reasoned evidence of the return to normalcy. I was unaccustomed to the wild screeches and screams, to the rubbish collectors; the silence of guns and canons was unsettling. I had no longing for the war, but was at a loss without its markers. Somehow the emotional surge of fear had dissipated from my memory, yet the sounds of gunfire had registered as the habitual noises of the night.

It took me a couple of years to stop feeling that estrangement with everyday things. Driving along thoroughfares, once ago notorious shooting ranges for snipers, going to sectors past the once-forbidding dividing line, lazing my gaze on countryside landscapes, as if seeing them for the first time. Rediscovering the country, interacting with folk from neighbourhoods and communities once ago sworn enemies. A street where years earlier I had witnessed a respectable man forced out of his car by thugs with Kalashnikovs, slapped, shoved to the sidewalk and his car 'confiscated', became the street where a paramour kissed me for the first time. Recanting the violent episode did not help to smooth the transition, nor even wrinkle out the incoherence. The green line, where many disappeared or perished, became itself a mundane major artery consistently afflicted with congestion. For the first two years, stuck in traffic, deafened by the cacophony of impatient car horns, I could not restrain my mind from wandering into its recent past. And there were the unfinished abandoned buildings…Their construction arrested during the war for one reason or another, their voluminous greyish-brown cement carcasses had sheltered fighters, friends and foes, alternately. Their ground and first floors buttressed with sandbags had been makeshift barracks, their roofs substitute control towers and sometimes, if underground levels provided, they had served as temporary prisons and torture chambers.

Tucked between finished buildings, where everyday people lived, they were edifying gruesome landmarks; I remember all too well how I looked away, intently, whenever I came across them, for fear my gaze might elicit the ire of a young man with a gun and license to the free exercise of heedless violence. These carcasses were idioms in the urban vocabulary of the civil war. Once it was over, they were evacuated fairly quickly. The Syrian army, which was mandated to police the transition from war to non-war, took over a few, they generally opted for less precarious shelters and squatted in buildings whose residents had simply deserted. Another few housed undocumented Syrian workers whose sorry luck had turned really sour. For the most part, unfinished buildings and their bulksome carcasses were left to abandon, forsaken. Theirs was the most radical of conversions, from chilling mileposts to unintelligible, morose presence. They were practically invisible now that they were of no use to anyone, so vexing a sight we preferred to dismiss. And those who lived in their carcasses, even in passing, became invisible, too.

Undocumented Syrian workers came in droves in the first few years of the end of the war. The unquantifiable, cheap labour, whose sweat enabled the (so-called) miracle, working atrocious hours, in injurious conditions for dishonest wages. Dirt-poor boys and men from the dirt-poor Syrian hinterland, looking to make a quick buck and to realise the promise of material promotion back home. They were sentenced to remain nameless, ignorant and suspicious, fulfilling the role of the 'inferior and hateful' group, feeding at the bottommost of our society.

Defenseless, they took the heat for the Syrian tutelage of the country. Besides the toxic intimacy of the Syrian regime with our conflicts and paradoxes, from the onset, the Syrian military had effectively an active presence on the stage and in the ever-unfolding drama of our civil war. The first round was in 1976, but that's a chapter too far removed to dwell on here; the second round involved deployment in the western flank of Beirut, in the second half of the 1980s, with a stealth mandate to restore some sort of order and to inhibit the Lebanese from ravenously murdering one another. Their strategy was basic: monopolise and upstage the ministrations of violence, indiscriminately. Their état-major took up residence in a hotel close to the seashore, ominously known as the Beau Rivage. The soldiers, however, established makeshift barracks close to checkpoints at intersections or on corners deemed 'strategic' in the ever-changing map of internecine fighting; they settled on the ground, first and second floors of apartment buildings emptied of their original residents over the span of the years of the civil war. They forced their way, none of the apartments was handed over.

Over the years, by force of habit, or by forcing habit, their barracking integrated into the fabric of the city. By the time the war ended, ad hoc garrisons became less and less impermanent, the purported time limit of their official mandate kept receding officiously further in the future. The post-war truce dictated a pullout; it was implemented in fits and starts over years, demurely. Essentially it was pointless because the military intelligence apparatus had struck firm root in the nooks and crannies of governance, permeating almost every single civil and uncivil transaction in the conduct of our lives. The post-war reconstruction and recovery miracle was a big get-rich-quick scheme for the country's political class and its affiliates in the Syrian junta. These sinister plots were never entirely secret, but the full scale of their unravelling remained mysterious, instead we were given official versions explaining why a contract was awarded to this and that consortium of companies, why monies allocated to a project had to be increased suddenly, why audits fell short of their missions, why new ministries were instituted, why national budgets were discussed in Damascus and so on and so forth. Official versions amounted to an official narrative, and an official vocabulary, idiom and grammar. The decoding was at times amusing and at times chilling, we learnt it mutatis mutandis, resigned to what seemed the de facto insuperable order of the day.

For as much as the war had its deafening soundscape of fire power exploding at all times of day and night, so did the post-war eventually claim its own soundscape, equally deafening, from reconstruction and construction. (It was an exclusively daytime soundtrack.) Once the advertising campaign's bombast grabbed hold of hearts and minds, investors, developers and the moneyed gentry of the war released, with frenzied enthusiasm, the means, machinery and droves of (undocumented) workers to restore Lebanon's former prosperity, mostly Beirut's. In spite of self-congratulating claims of patriotic disposition, they too saw a get-rich-quick business opportunity. Construction sites mushroomed every day, everywhere, like an epidemic, and there was no overarching supervision to coordinate and reason private initiative, or to defend abuses of public rights. Planning, land use, scale, measure, architectural character, all the yardsticks for a studied growth and safeguarding quality of the living environment, were summarily forsaken. Beirut had much catching up to do, and delaying the momentum was a luxury the country could not afford, we were told.

I remember waking up bleary-eyed to the thundering thumps of mechanical earth-diggers, bobcats with long appendages that ended with metal teeth and plumbed Beirut's hard rock underbelly. There was a grim ferocity to their repetitive persistence, the concrete pouring tirelessly, promising congestion rather than prosperity. For whom were they being built? It did not really matter, 'build and they will come' said the chorus of officialdom. It turned out that the high-luxury, spanking-new buildings were intended for moneyed Arabs to whom Beirut and Lebanon were handed over as a second home. The mid-range, luxury new buildings were intended for expatriate Lebanese to whom fortune had been kind in their lives abroad. The modest buildings, intended for us, everyday folk, sprouted at the outer rims of the outer rims of Beirut, eastward, westward, southward and northward. Those of us natives and residents, who had stayed, were summoned to move to the 'new' suburbs, where basic amenities such as water, electricity and sewage were not accommodating yet. That was our lot in the miraculous recovery.

And that was not all of it. We, those who stayed in the country, steadfast and foolhardy during the long drama of our uncivil war, those who had been left behind, it turns out, had really been left behind in the general forward-moving progress of the world...We had some serious catching up to do, if we were to reclaim Lebanon's place as the unique encounter of East and West on the map, and the First World service economy in the badlands of the 'developing world'. We had to sharpen antiquated skills, and update our fledgling command over information and technology, tune up to hot trends, wake up to the call of postmodernity...We had to catch up to the expatriates who were returning with fancy university degrees and refined training of sub

sub-specialties. They were the genial navigators assigned to the vanguard of steering us through this miraculous recovery. Under their pilotship, the ship would not sink again into civil conflict, we were told, as we, survivors of the cataclysm, boastful with the pride of survivors, were suddenly pushed aside and below. We were maimed, scarred, tainted, and it showed – we carried burdens of the past, our gait betrayed it – meanwhile, the expatriates had been reprogrammed or deprogrammed in their time outside the country.

The war would never happen again, officials parading on television insisted in various speech acts. There was a refrain: 'The Lebanese will never make war again, they have learnt their lesson, the war is behind us all'. Their self-assurance was at once impressive and worrisome. Were they delusional or illusionists? On the one hand, we were meant to believe that we were a people who loved peace far more than war, and on the other hand, we were fragile enough that we needed the mentorship of our neighbouring Syrian regime to assist us in the transition from war to peace. It stopped to matter at some point who believed what – decoding the rhetoric lost its relevance. We had to get by. They were right that most people preferred non-war, and that everyone, fighters and their families, victims and their families, innocent bystanders and their families, we, them, all of us, had emerged from this prolonged war worn out, exhausted. The respite, whether presented as delusion or illusion, was not unwelcome.

Move forward, focus on the future, no point dwelling on the past. Forget the past in order to live in the present and imagine the future; if we force a forgetting now, the future will become nearer, ours for the taking. In time, the forgetting will feel natural. Repeat any set of instructions enough times and they acquire the gravitas of maxims or popular wisdom. Maybe that's what happened. For those first couple of years, we were summoned to become like returnees to our country, feigning an amnesia to enable that liberating travel in time: find the Lebanon of 1975 or 1974 or 1973 retouched, retold, reconstructed, and build the present moment from within it, the Lebanon of 1994 ,1993 ,1992... Erasing the traces of our war, stowing away grief, moving past scars. I remember how the everyday furnishings of war-time survival fell into disuse, transformed to clutter and eventually got discarded or packed away – the plastic gallon-sized containers that stored gasoline or fuel for generators, the many-shaped battery-operated lights, the stock of several-sized batteries, the dozen photocopies of identity papers, the many-sized portable radios...Listening compulsively to the radio news broadcast at hourly or half-hourly intervals, zapping from the version of allies to the version of enemies.

The post-war agreement contained no master plan for the conversion from war to non-war, except for an amnesty law that allowed the once-warlords to people the executive and legislative bodies of the republic. It was up to civil society to propose a scheme for the closure, some kind of a restorative if not retributive justice, a truth and reconciliation commission, short of a war crimes tribunal. Trouble was, the warlords-cum-democratic representatives were supposed to usher the first phase of the transition and retire. They never did, and we did not manage to oust them. Instead, many, many, 'conflict resolution' conferences were organised, where experts, local and international, presented papers and spoke with eloquence, but discussion systematically hit a wall. Some of the most marginalised political protagonists in the post-war published memoirs; at worst they were disingenuous mea culpas, at best exquisite literary works of probing, self-critical autobiography. Amnesty fomented a whimsical form of amnesia, selective not in what it opted to forget, but when it chose to remember. Redemption and forgiving were perhaps more paradoxical and confused, some militia fighters voluntarily confessed to hate and killing, redeeming their new life in the post-war. Even if their audience was ambivalent about granting a pardon, the penchant was widely overrun by pragmatism, prodding a discussion on past wounds, and hurt was widely perceived as poking fingers into a nasty can of worms, better to avoid at the present moment. Amnesia induced relief. Maybe we were buying time, sure, but we, people, needed the let-up. In the first few years after the war had officially ended, a euphoric amnesia, almost manic, gripped a great deal of people. Some of us, others, me, did not quite know how to keep up.

Euphoria emulsified into excess. Looking svelte and attractive, for example, became a collective obsession, gyms were gradually packed to the seams and extended hours of operation, plastic surgeons worked overtime, investing in personal styling became evidence of bounty, physical and mental...Living large, binging and flaunting it, were celebrated alternately as restorative and retributive. At the risk of indulging pop-psychology, there must have been an element of compensation for the years of youth lost during the war, and perhaps as well an element of reversing or recuperating from the damage of the war. Stories abound of passionate adultery, lurid orgies, exorbitantly lavish parties, eventually the glossy magazines that chronicled – in photos mostly – the bold and the beautiful as they fêted themselves, their anniversaries, weddings or even the return of spring, sold like hot cakes. The once-defenseless but morally upright victims, thus self-congratulating heroes, became fit, toned, supercilious and even more self-righteous. You don't survive a civil war by virtue of your merit; almost invariably, you avoid death by sheer luck, felicitous happenstance or calibrated caution. I remember being infected by the euphoria in fits – I did not manage to transform my body according to the new standards, nor was I haunted with catching up on lost years and occasions for merriment.

I remember surrendering every once in a while to the calling of amnesia and feeling relief from the weight of things past, momentarily. I was nonetheless a maladroit convert. I was not alone, I knew that well; there were others, maladroit, ill at ease or simply skeptical. They were more obviously ambivalent, broken and out of place. It's not that the war had provide them (or us) a place, rather, we neither bought into the government's plan for the post-war, nor did we possess the wherewithal or motivation to transform ourselves into new versions of ourselves. We dragged our feet in the frenzied rush forward.

Some people's destinies had been derailed by the war. Everyday ambitions, dreams of self-realisation, simple plans such as attending medical school, becoming an artist, marrying a school sweetheart, buying a house to make a home, finding a job with a salary and securities were pushed off-track. The violence forced people to reconsider these matters, to make compromise after compromise to get by in the immediate future. Defer plans until the situation improved, or the enemy was defeated, or the conspiracy foiled, or the war ended. As years went by, more compromises had to be made, some had to move to neighbourhoods they deemed safer, or because they no longer had a home; some had to drop out of school to fend for their lives or support their families after the death of a parent; some chose to take leave of civilian life and answer the call of duty to fight. That derailment eventually became a fact of life, of the everyday, and dreams of making something of one's life were folded and packed into oblivion. The warring was not continuous, there had been rounds of violence and lulls, children went to school, commerce and trade were active, cinemas screened films and pastry chefs created new desserts, but the opportunities for making something meaningful of one's life shrank over these long, grief-stricken years. The austerity and sorrow of survival took hold. The end of the war was in principle a chance at a fresh start. In the conversion from fighter, victim, innocent bystander, survivor, hero, to citizen, we were all given a chance at a fresh start to become a new version of ourselves fashioned in our own hands, on our own terms. For almost all of us, by the time the war ended, it was often too late to pick up seriously from the instance of that derailment. Too much had happened in the meantime. The electrician who had dreamed of becoming an engineer at age eighteen, when the war broke out, and worked alternately as an electrician, ran a small shop, then assisted a friend in his house calls for electrical repairs and eventually again as an electrician, did not even consider pursuing a new life as an engineer at the end of the war. The secretary who dreamed of medical school but lost her father halfway through the war and had to support her mother and younger siblings immediately, did not even contemplate going to medical school after the war ended. The butcher who inherited his father's shop and craft, and entertained friends and neighbours playing the 'ud on quiet nights, laughed bitterly when asked if he would try to perform in public places and take his talent seriously.

Between amnesty, amnesia, euphoria and the sinister spectre of belligerence looming on our horizon, invisible yet tangible, I remember feeling estranged, out of place, in the present, of these first years of the return to normalcy. The dead were gone for good, the missing remained for a persistent absence; roads were fixed, each at least twice or three times in merely three or four years; ravaged buildings were knocked down or spackled, the traces of our conflict became a badge of dishonour; schools were revamped but the national curriculum did not include the

Hotel, Rmeyleh, built in 2003

فندق في الرميلة، بني عام 2003

Holiday Inn Hotel, Minet el-Hosn, built in 1970 – 1973

فندق هوليدي إن، مينا الحصن، بني عام 1970 – 1973

Current page: The Saint Georges Hotel, Ain el-Mreisseh, built in 1950
Facing page: Côte d'Azur Hotel, Jnah, built in 1973

الصفحة الحالية: فندق سان جورج، عين المريسة، بُني عام 1950
الصفحة المقابلة: فندق الكوت دازور، جناح، بُني عام 1973

war in history books; instead of bringing closure, for lack of genuine motive and political will, the war was suspended in a realm between forgetting and trauma. In the early years of our post-war, it became clear that it would be our extraordinarily missed opportunity at innovating, repairing, recovering and building a country, albeit hostage to the paradoxes of the region, but genuinely civil, humane, clement and novel. Our bereavement might have been the starting point for reversing the horror and pain; equal opportunities for acquiring new skills and changing one's life might have unburdened the dark weight of the legacy of the war; grief might have been exhumed collectively; new rituals and traditions might have acknowledged loss; the lot of unfinished, abandoned buildings could have transformed into libraries, archives, spaces for creative production or affordable housing, their legacy of terror and torture turned on its head. Such initiatives were furthest removed from the mindset and calculus of our government, political class, intelligentsia and civil society. It was not a failure of collective imagination, rather the dead weight of bereavement and blinding paradoxes of our post-war. Bereft, we were, taking every day as it came, bracing for the worst, deafened by the thunders of construction sites, frenzied to catch up, whimsical amnesiacs and giddy.

Close to fifteen years after the war ended, and thirty years after it broke out, the cycle of violence erupted again.

Facing page: Building 9, Fouad Chehab ring road, Ashrafieh, 1971 – 1979

الصفحة المقابلة: بناية التسعة (9)، جسر فؤاد شهاب، بنيت عام 1971 – 1979

Current page: Hotel Chalouhi, Zalka, built in 1985
Facing page: Building intended to be a hotel, Zalka, built in 1988 – 1989

الصفحة الحالية: فندق الشالوحي، الزلقا، بني عام 1985
الصفحة المقابلة: فندق بدون اسم، الزلقا، بني عام 1988 – 1989

Building in Jdeydet el-Metn, built in 1997 – 1998

بناية في الجديدة، بنيت عام 1997 – 1998

34

Current and facing pages: Building in Ain el-Tineh, destroyed in 2007
Previous page: Hilton Beirut Hotel, Hamra, built in 1998

الصفحة الحالية والصفحة المقابلة: بناية في عين التينة، دمرت عام 2007
الصفحة التالية: فندق هيلتون، الحمرا، بني عام 1998

Current page: Hotel Mirador, Khaldeh, built in 1960 – 1963
Facing page: Building in Corniche el-Nahr, between Borj Hammoud and Sin el-Fil

Building in Jnah

بناية في جناح

Social Security Building, Fouad Chehab ring road, built in 1970

بناية الضمان، جسر فؤاد شهاب، بنيت عام 1970

Saliba Building, Jal el-Dib, built in 1988

بناية صليبا، جل الديب، بنيت عام 1988

44

Current page: The Suqs Building, Jnah, built in 1983
Facing page: James Building, Zalka, built in 1983

الصفحة الحالية: بناية الأسواق، جناح، بنيت عام 1983
الصفحة المقابلة: بناية جايمز، الزلقا، بنيت عام 1983

Fattoush Building, Hazmieh, built in 1996

بناية فتوش، الحازمية، بنيت عام 1996

Current and facing page: Paladium Building, Hamra, built in 1981
Following page: Al-Batrakiyyeh (The Patriarchate), Jezzin (south Lebanon), circa 1930s

الصفحةالحالية والمقابلة: بناية بالاديوم، الحمرا، بنيت عام 1981
الصفحة السابقة: بناية البطركية، جزين، بنيت في الثلاثينيات

شاليهات فندق الكوت دازور، جناح، بني عام 1973

Châlets of Côte d'Azur Hotel, Jnah, built in 1973

Current page: Murr Tower, Wadi Abu Jmil, built in 1973
Facing page: Paladium Building, Hamra, built in 1981

الصفحة الحالية: برج المر، وادي أبو جميل، بني عام 1973
الصفحة المقابلة: بناية بالاديوم، الحمرا، بنيت عام 1981

Current page: Cote d'Azur Hotel, Jnah, built in 1973
Facing page: Building in Jnah, built in 1970

الصفحة الحالية: فندق الكوت دازور، جناح، بني عام 1973
الصفحة المقابلة: بناية في جناح، بنيت عام 1970

Current page: Building in Dohet el-Hoss, built in 1978 – 1979
Facing and previous page: Building in Wardiyeh

الصفحة الحالية: بناية في دوحة الحص، بنيت عام 1978 – 1979
الصفحة المقابلة والصفحة السابقة: بناية في الوردية

The Germans Building, Jnah, built in 1980

بناية الألمان، جناح، بنيت عام 1980

Current page: Building in Clemémenceau street (Qantari), built in 1980s
Facing page: Building in Wardiyeh

الصفحة الحالية: بناية في شارع كليمنصو (القنطاري)، بنيت في الثمانينيات
الصفحة المقابلة: بناية في الوردية

View of Raousheh from Ramlet el-Bayda

مشهد للروشة من الرملة البيضاء

Current page: Spinney's, Ramlet el-Bayda, built in 1970
Facing page: Building in Jeitawi (Ashrafieh)

الصفحة الحالية: بناية سبينيز، الرملة البيضاء، بنيت عام 1970
الصفحة المقابلة: بناية في الجعيتاوي (الأشرفية)

Building in Jiyyeh, south Lebanon

بناية في الجية، جنوب لبنان

الصفحة الحالية: مطاحن سنّو، كورنيش النهر، بنيت في الخمسينيات
الصفحة المقابلة: بناية في ضبية

Current page: Sinno Mills, Corniche el-Nahr, built in the 1950s
Facing page: Building in Dbayeh

Current page: Building in Ramlet el-Bayda, built in 1970
Facing page: Dar el-Elm Publishing Building, Fouad Chehab ring road, built in 1970

الصفحة الحالية: بناية في الرملة البيضاء، بنيت عام 1970
الصفحة المقابلة: بناية دار العلم للملايين، جسر فؤاد شهاب، بنيت عام 1970

Spinney's, Ramlet el-Bayda, built in 1970

بناية سبينيز، الرملة البيضاء، بنيت عام 1970

Building in Ashrafieh, built in 1992

بناية في الأشرفية، بنيت عام 1992

Current page:Building in Caracas
Facing page: Building in Qantari, built in 2004
Previous page: Khayyat Building, Wata al-Musaytbeh, built in 1983

الصفحة الحالية: بناية في كاراكاس
الصفحة المقابلة:بناية في القنطاري، بنيت عام 2004
الصفحة التالية: بناية الخياط، وطى المصيطبة، بنيت عام 1983

Current page: Building in Dohet el-Hoss, built in 1978 – 1979
Facing page: Murr Tower, Wadi Abu Jmil, built in 1973
Following page: Building in Ashrafieh, built in 1992

الصفحة الحالية: بناية في دوحة الحص، بنيت عام 1978 – 1979
الصفحة المقابلة: برج المر، وادي أبو جميل، بني عام 1973
الصفحة السابقة: بناية في الأشرفية، بنيت عام 1992

Current page: Building in Saloumeh
Facing page: Carlton Tower Hotel, Raousheh, built in 1987

الصفحة الحالية: بناية في صالومي
الصفحة المقابلة: فندق برج الكارلتون، الروشة، بني عام 1987

The Lybian Hospital, Ramlet el-Bayda, built in 1970

المستشفى الليبي، الرملة البيضاء، بنيت عام 1970

مصائر الناس كانت قد حادت خلال الحرب. التطلعات اليومية، أحلام تحقيق الذات، خطط بسيطة مثل الالتحاق بكلية الطب أو كلية الفنون، الزواج من حبيبة أيام الدراسة، شراء منزل لتكوين أسرة، إيجاد عمل بدخل مُناسب، كل هذا حاد عن طريقه. العنف أجبر الناس على إعادة النظر في هذه الأمور الحاضرة وأن يقبلوا بحلول وسط وتنازلات إلى أن يمضي هذا الحاضر. تأجيل الخطط حتى يتحسن الوضع أو ينهزم العدو أو تنكشف المؤامرة أو تنتهي الحرب. مع مرور السنين ازدادت التنازلات، بعض الناس اضطروا لأن ينتقلوا لأحياء يعتبرونها أكثر أمناً، أو لأنهم فقدوا منازلهم؛ بعض الطلبة تركوا دراستهم حتى يُعيلوا أسرهم بعدما مات مُعيلهم الأساسي؛ البعض اختار أن يترك الحياة المدنية ويستجيب لدعوة القتال. هذا الحيود أصبح جزءاً من الحياة اليومية، أحلام تحقيق الذات طُويّت وصارت طي النسيان. الاقتتال لم يكن مُتواصل، فترات العنف كانت تتخللها فترات هدوء، الأطفال كانوا يذهبون إلى مدارسهم، التجارة والاقتصاد كانا يعملان، السينمات تعرض الأفلام، صانعو الحلوى ابتكروا أصنافاً جديدة، ولكن فُرَص أن يصنع المرء شيئاً ذا معنى بحياته تَضَاءلت كثيراً طوال سنين الحرب الحزينة. التقشف والأسى ازدادا بسبب الرغبة في النجاة. نهاية الحرب كانت من حيث المبدأ فرصة لبداية جديدة. في التحول من مُقاتل، ضحية، شاهد عيان، ناج، بطل.. إلى مُواطن، كُلنا أُعطينا فرصة لبداية أخرى لنصنع من أنفسنا شخصيات جديدة بأيدينا ومَراجعنا. عندما انتهت الحرب كان الوقت قد تأخر بالنسبة لمُعظمنا لكي يعود إلى لحظة ما قبل الحيود. لقد حدث الكثير منذ ذلك الحين. عامل الكهرباء الذي كان يحلم أن يكون مُهندساً وهو في سن الثامنة عشرة عندما اندلعت الحرب والذي عمل تارة كعامل كهرباء ثم أدار دكاناً ثم صار يُساعد صديقاً في أعماله الكهربائية في ورشات خارجية ثم عاد إلى عمله بعدها، إنه لم يتوقف بعد الحرب ليسعى إلى حياة جديدة كمهندس. السكرتيرة التي حلمت بكلية الطب ولكنها فقدت أبيها وسط الحرب واضطرت لإعالة أمها وأخوتها الصغار فوراً، لم تُفكر للحظة في العودة لكلية الطب عندما انتهت الحرب. والجزار الذي ورث مهنة أبيه ودكانه والذي كان يُسلي الأصدقاء والجيران بعزف العود في الليالي الهادئة، كان يضحك بمرارة عندما لا يُسئل إذا كان يرغب في العزف على العود في الأماكن العامة ويتعامل مع موهبته بجدية.

بين العفو وفقدان الذاكرة وبين النشوة وبين طيف الحرب المريب الذي كان يُحلق في الأفق، أتذكر كيف كُنت أشعر بالغربة وعدم الانتماء للمكان في السنوات الأولى للعودة للحياة العادية. الموتى كانوا قد رحلوا إلى الأبد، والمخطوفون أصبحوا هم الغياب الحاضر؛ الطرقات كانت قد أُصلحت، كل طريق تم اصلاحه على الأقل مرّتين أو ثلاثة في غضون ثلاث أو أربع سنوات؛ الأبنية المُدمرة إما تمت إزالتها أو تم ترميمها أصبحت شهادات عدم شرف. تم تجديد المدارس ولكن المناهج الدراسية الوطنية لم تشمل الحرب في كتب التاريخ؛ عوضاً عن إنجاز تتمة للحرب وبسبب عدم وجود غاية صادقة وإرادة سياسية أصبحت الحرب مُعلقة في فضاء ما بين النسيان و"التروما". في السنين الأولى لما بعد الحرب أصبح واضحاً أنها ستكون فرصة ضائعة هائلة من الإبداع والتصحيح والشفاء وبناء بلد إنساني رحيم متطور ومتحضر حتى ولو كان أسيراً لتناقضات المنطقة. بكُلنا كان من الممكن أن يكون نقطة بداية لقلب أوضاع الألم والهلع؛ فرص متساوية لاكتساب مهارات جديدة وتغيير حياتنا حتى يستطيع المرء أن يتخلص من الثقل الأسود لإرث الحرب؛ كان مُمكناً التخلص من الأسى الذي في داخلنا؛ تقاليد وعادات وطقوس جديدة كان يُمكن أن تُبتكر للتعويض عن الشعور بالفقدان؛ الأبنية غير المكتملة والمهجورة كان من الممكن تحويلها إلى مكتبات وأرشيفات وأماكن إبداع ومساكن زهيدة الثمن، إرثهم من الرعب والتعذيب هكذا يُعاد تدويره. كل هذه المبادرات كانت على أبعد مسافة من عقلية الحكومة والطبقة السياسية والمثقفين والمجتمع المدني. لم يكن الفشل على مستوى المخيلة الجماعية، لكن آثار وزن الثقل المُميت وتناقضات ما بعد الحرب التي تُعمي. كنا نتعامل مع كل يوم ونحن نُكل، متأهبون للأسوأ. مصدوعون من ضجيج ورشات الإعمار، مهرولون كي نُعوض عن تخلفنا، فاقدون للذاكرة بمزاجية ومُنتشون.

تقريباً بعد خمسة عشر عاماً من إعلان نهاية الحرب، وبعد ثلاثين عاماً من اندلاعها، انفجرت موجة العنف مرة أخرى.

هذا لم يكن كل شيء. نحن الذين اخترنا البقاء في البلد بولعنا الساذج وصمودنا، تحملنا الدراما الطويلة لحربنا الأهلية التي لا أهلية فيها، نحن الذين تخلفنا في الوطن، تبدى لنا تخلفنا عن مواكبة التطور العالمي... كان هناك الكثير لنحصله، إذا كنا نريد أن نستعيد مكانة لبنان الفريدة كنقطة التقاء بين الشرق والغرب واقتصاد واقتصاد خدمات من مستوى العالم الأول في منطقة الدول النامية. كان لزاماً علينا أن نُجدد مهاراتنا ونُحدث كيفية سيطرتنا على المعرفة والتكنولوجيا، ونُحسن إلمامَنا بأحدث خطوط الموضة، ونستيقظ لدعوة ما بعد الحداثة... كان علينا أن نطور أنفسنا كي نواكب المغتربين العائدين بشهاداتهم من الجامعات الفاخرة، والخبرات دقيقة التخصص. كانوا هم الطليعة العبقرية التي كُلّفت بقيادة معجزة التعافي. تحت قيادتهم لم يكن هناك أي خطر من أن يغرق القارب في أي صراع أهلي، هكذا قيل لنا. وبينما كنا نحن الذين نجونا من المصيبة نمتلئ فخراً بنجاتنا، فجأة صرنا على الهامش، مشوهين، مليئين بالندبات (وكان هذا واضحاً) كنا ننوء بحمل الماضي بينما كان قد أعيد تأهيل المغتربين باغترابهم هذا.

لن تكن هناك مرة ثانية، الرسميون كانوا يؤكدون بإصرار على ذلك في التلفاز، كان الكوبليه الدائم: "اللبنانيون لن يُحاربوا ثانيةً، لقد تعلموا الدرس، الحرب صارت وراءنا" ثقتهم بأنفسهم كانت مؤثرة كما كانت مُقلقة، هل كانوا يخدعون أنفسهم أم كانوا لنا خادعون؟ في نفس الوقت طُلب منا أن نُصدق أننا أناسٌ نُفضّل السلم على الحرب، وأن إيماننا ضعيفاً بالقدر الذي كنا معه في حاجة إلى نظام شقيق لينقلنا من حالة الحرب إلى حالة السلم. بعد فترة لم يعد مهماً من يُصدق ماذا. فك شفرة الخطابات والاستذكاء عليها لم يعد له معنى. كان لزاماً علينا أن ندع الحياة تمر. كانوا على حق في ظنهم أن مُعظم الناس لا يحبون الحرب، وأن المُقاتلين وعائلاتهم، الضحايا وعائلاتهم، شهود العيان وعائلاتهم، نحن، هم، كلنا، جميعنا خرجنا من هذه الحرب الطويلة مُرهقين. حتى أننا قبلنا أن يكون ثمن الراحة المشروعة هو أن نكون مخدوعين.

سر إلى الأمام، ركز على المستقبل، انس الماضي، لا جدوى من التعلق بالماضي، إذا اصطنعنا النسيان الآن فإن المستقبل سيبدو أقرب وفي المُتناول، أما النسيان فسيبدو مع الوقت طبيعياً. إذا كرّرتْ هذه التعليمات مرات كافية فإنها ستتحول إلى حكم ومأثورات، ويبدو أن هذا ما حدث فعلاً. في تلك السنوات الأولى كنا مدفوعين إلى التصرف كأننا عائدون إلى بلدنا، نصطنع فقداناً للذاكرة حتى يسهل علينا التحرك عبر الزمن كي نُلاقي لبنان سنوات 1975، 74، 73 لكن مع بعض الرتوش التي نبني من خلالها في هذه اللحظة من الحاضر لبنان في سنوات 1992، 93، 94... أن نمحي آثار الحرب ونُلْمْلِمْ أحزاننا ونتخطى الجروح. أتذكر كيف أن الأشياء التي كنا نستخدمها في أيام الحرب لم يعد لها أية ضرورة مُهملة وتحولت إلى مُخلّفات، بعد فترة لمْلمناها وألقيناها.. "الجالونات" البلاستيكية التي كنا نعبئها بوقود المولدات، الكشافات التي تعمل بالبطاريات الجافة على اختلاف أحجامها، مخزون البطاريات بأحجامها المتعددة، استنساخات الهويات، الراديوهات بأشكال مُختلفة... مُلاحقة نشرة الأخبار بهَوَس كل ساعة أو كل نصف ساعة والتنقل بين محطات الحلفاء ومحطات الأعداء لمتابعة الأحداث.

الاتفاق الذي أنهى الحرب لم يكن مُتضمناً على خطة عامة للانتقال من حالة الحرب إلى حالة اللا حرب لكن كان هناك قانون العفو الذي سمح لأمراء الحرب أن ينفذوا إلى الجسد التشريعي والتنفيذي للجمهورية. كان من المفروض على المجتمع المدني أن يقترح خطة للإنهاء، شيء من العدالة التي تُصحح ولا تَقْتص، أو على الأقل شيء ما يُشبه "لجنة التحقيق والمصالحة"، بدلاً عن محكمة لجرائم الحرب. كانت المشكلة أن أمراء الحرب الذين أصبحوا المُمثّلين الديمُقراطيين أصبحوا هم أنفسهم المسؤولين عن المرحلة الأولى من الانتقال ومن ثم يتقاعدون بعد ذلك. لم يفعلوا، ونحن لم نستطع إزاحتهم، وبدلاً عن ذلك عُقد الكثير والكثير من المؤتمرات عن موضوع حل الصراعات. حيث كان الخبراء محليين ودوليين يقدمون أوراق العمل ويتكلمون ببراعة، ولكن النقاشات كان يتم الإلقاء بها في عرض الحائط. بعض الشخصيات السياسية من الذين هُمّشُوا فيما بعد الحرب نشروا مُذكراتهم؛ في أسوأ الأحوال كانت هذه المذكرات اعترافات غير صادقة وفي أحسن الأحوال كانت أعمالاً أدبية من النقد الذاتي والسيرة الذاتية. قانون العفو أفرز نوعاً من فقدان الذاكرة غير المألوف، لم يكن انتقائياً في نسيان الأشياء ولكنه كان انتقائياً في متى نتذكر هذه الأشياء. الغفران والعفو كانا أكثر تناقضاً من هذا التشويش، البعض من مُقاتلي الميليشيات اعترفوا عن طواعية بالكره والقتل. كأنهم كانوا يريدون تطهير أنفسهم بالاعتراف حتى يبدؤوا حياه جديدة فيما بعد الحرب. حتى ولو كان جمهورهم مُحَيّراً فيما إذا كان ينبغي عليه أن يُسامحهم. كانت البراجماتية هي الاتجاه السائد، بمعنى أن افتعال أي نقاش عن جروح وآلام الماضي كان يُنظر إليه على أنه اصطياد في الماء العكر ومن الأفضل تفاديه في الوقت الحاضر. فقدان الذاكرة هذا خلق ارتياحاً. بالتأكيد كنا نريح وقتاً ولكن نحن الناس كنا بحاجة إلى فسحة من التنفس. في هذه السنين الأولى، بعد أن انتهت الحرب بشكل رسمي. نشوة فُقدان الذاكرة أصابت الكثيرين. والبعض الآخر، وأنا منهم، لم نكن نعرف كيف نلحق بهم في نشوتهم.

الشعور بالنشوة سبّب إفراطاً. فمثلاً، أصبح هناك هوس أن يكون الشخص رشيقاً وجذاباً، النوادي الرياضية أصبحت مُزدحمة وزيدت ساعات العمل بها، جراحو التجميل صاروا يعملون أوقاتاً إضافية، الاعتناء المبالغ فيه بالمظهر الخارجي. كل هذه الأشياء كانت تُعتبر دليل الوجاهة الجسدية والنفسية... البذخ والنهم والاستعراض كانت أحياناً هي أعراض التعافي أو التعويض. أرغب في تجنب التحليل النفسي السطحي لكن بالتأكيد كان هناك شيء من التعويض عن سنوات الشباب التي فُقدت خلال الحرب، وربما أيضاً كان هناك شيء ما من المقابل عن الخراب الذي نتج عن الحرب. كانت هناك حكايات كثيرة عن خيانات زوجية ماجنة، ليالي حمراء مبتذلة، حفلات سفيهة. في الصحف والمجلات البراقة التي كانت تُتابع (بالصور فقط) كيف أن المجتمع المخملي كان يحتفل بنفسه وأعياده وأفراحه أو حتى بعودة الربيع، هذه الصحافة صارت مُزدهرة جداً. الضحايا الذين كانوا لفترة ضعفاء رغم كونهم على حق والذين كانوا يعتبرون أنفسهم أبطالاً أصبحوا هم الوسيمين والرشقاء فازدادوا إحساساً بأنهم معصومون عن الخطأ. لا أحد ينجو من حرب أهلية بمهارته، إنهم عموماً يتفادون الموت إما بالحظ الحسن أو بالأقدار الرحيمة أو بالحذر الشديد. أتذكر أنه قد أصابني مس من هذا الشعور والنشوة، لم أستطع تحويل جسدي للمقاييس الجديدة ولم أكن مهووسة بالتعويض عن سنين ضائعة أو عن فُرص للمرح. أتذكر أني كنت أحياناً أستسلم لفقدان الذاكرة وأرتاح من ثقل الأشياء الفائتة. كنت من الذين يعانون أثناء تحولهم. لم أكن وحيدة. كنت أعلم جيداً أن هناك آخرين، الذين كانت حيرتهم أكثر وضوحاً مني والذين كانوا معطوبين وخارج المكان. الموضوع لم يكن أن الحرب قد أعطتنا مكان، على العكس، لم نكن نؤمن بخطة الحكومة لما بعد الحرب، ولم يكن لدينا الأدوات أو الدوافع كي نحول أنفسنا إلى صيغة جديدة من أنفسنا. ففي هرولة الجمع إلى الأمام كنا نُجرجر أرجلنا.

إعادة اكتشاف البلد، التفاعل مع ناس من أحياء وجماعات كانت فيما قبل أعداء لدودة. منذ سنين خلت كنت مارة عبر شارع عندما رأيت رجلاً ذا مظهر محترم تجره مجموعة من البلطجية يحملون الكلاشنكوف، يصفعونه ويرمون به إلى طرف الرصيف ثم يستولون على سيارته. هذا الشارع هو نفسه الآن الذي قبلي فيه حبيب للمرة الأولى. استعادة ذكرى هذه الحادثة العنيفة والبوح بها لم يساعدني أبداً على تسهيل الموقف ولا الحد من التنافر. الخط الأخضر (الذي كان يقسم بيروت إلى نصفيها الشرقي والغربي) حيث العديدون اختُطفوا أو لقوا حتفهم، صار هو أيضاً جادة أساسية، دائماً مزدحمة. في السنتين الأوليتين فيما بعد الحرب كنت عندما أكون عالقة في زحامها ويعلو نفير السيارات فأني لم أكن أستطيع منع نفسي من تذكر ماضيها القريب. وكانت الأبنية المهجورة غير مكتملة البناء، التي قد توقف العمل فيها أثناء الحرب لسبب ما، هياكلها الأسمنتية الثقيلة الرمادية والبنية قد أوت المقاتلين، حلفاء أو أعداء بشكل متوال. الطوابق الأرضية والأولى المُدعمة بأكياس الرمل كانت قد تكونت فيها ثكنات، أسطحها تحولت إلى أبراج مُراقبة، وإذا ما كانت هذه المباني تحتوي على طوابق أسفل الأرض فأنها تحولت إلى سجون مؤقتة أو أماكن للتعذيب.

مدسوسة بين مباني عامرة حيث كانت الناس تعيش حياتها العادية، كانت هذه المباني معالم مُريبة. أتذكر بوضوح كيف كنت أحول نظري عنها مُتعمدة عندما أمر بجانبها خوفاً من أن أستفز بنظرتي شاباً يحمل مسدساً ويُعطي لنفسه الحق في أن يُمارس العنف دون مُبرر أو رادع. كانت هذه الأبنية جزءاً من اللغة المدينية للحرب الأهلية. ولما انتهت الحرب، صارت مهجورة بسرعة. الجيش السوري كُلّف بتأمين الانتقال من حالة الحرب إلى حالة اللا حرب، واستولى على بعض من هذه الأبنية. لكن بشكل عام كان الجنود يختارون مأوى أقل هشاشة وفضلوا البقاء في الأبنية العامرة التي هجرها سُكانها. البناءات غير المُكتملة تُركت مُهملة، وفي بعض الأحيان كان يسكن بعضها عمال سوريون تخلى الحظ عنهم ويقيمون بطريقة غير شرعية. على العموم فإن هذه الأبنية غير المُكتملة وهذه الهياكل المتثاقلة تُركت للإهمال. كان تَحوُّلها من كونها معالم تُثير الجزع إلى حضور مُبهم وكئيب هو التحول الأكثر حدة. بالكاد تكون مرئية. كأنها اختفت بسبب هُجرانها، مشهد كئيب لدرجة أننا كنا نتغاضى عنه. الذين كانوا يعيشون في هذه الهياكل حتى ولو بشكل عابر بالكاد أصبحوا مرئيين أيضاً. كأنهم اختفوا معها.

عمال سوريون غير شرعيين أتوا جحافل في أوائل سنين ما بعد الحرب. اليد العاملة الرخيصة والتي لم تنل حظها من أي أحصاء رسمي، هي التي صنعت معجزة إعادة الإعمار بكدها وعرقها، وهي التي كانت تعمل لساعات طويلة من القسوة في ظروف مُهينة بأجور مُذلّة. فتية ورجال من الريف السوري الذي يرتع فيه الفقر المُدقع جاؤوا سعياً وراء الكسب المادي، موعودين بالترقي عند عودتهم إلى بلدهم، كان محكوماً عليهم بأن يكونوا مجهولي الهوية، موصومين بالجهل، مشبوهين. ألبسوا دور الفئة المتدنية والكريهة في المجتمع.

لم يكن لديهم أية دفاعات، حملوا عبء كره الناس للجيش السوري. وفضلاً عن العلاقة الضالة بين النظام السوري وبين صراعاتنا وتناقضاتنا، فإنه كان هناك وجود فعلي للجيش السوري في ساحة دراما الحرب الأهلية. أول فصل من هذا الوجود كان عام 1976 وهو تاريخ جديد زمنياً ولن نتحدث عنه. أما الفصل الثاني فقد اقتضى انتشار فعلي في الطرف الغربي لبيروت في مُنتصف الثمانينيات حيث كان مُكلفاً بمهمة إعادة النظام، وردع اللبنانيين عن قتل بعضهم البعض. كانت استراتيجيتهم بسيطة وهي احتكار العنف والتباهي به ضد كل الناس. استوطنت القيادة العسكرية في فندق يقع على شاطئ البحر، وهو فندق البوريفاج، أما الجنود فقد أنشؤوا ثكناتهم البديلة بالقرب من الحواجز على تقاطعات طرق تُعتّبر استراتيجية في الخارطة المُتغيرة للقتال. قبعوا بالطوابق الأرضية والأدوار الأولى والثانية وأحياناً الثالثة في الأبنية التي نزح منها سكانها خلال سنوات الحرب الأهلية. اقتحموها بالقوة، لم تُمْنَح لهم.

على طول السنين ويحكم العادة أصبحت الثكنات جزءاً من نسيج المدينة، وعندما انتهت الحرب صارت هذه الثكنات البديلة غير مؤقتة، وطالت المهلة الزمنية لمهمتهم الرسمية إلى مدى غير محدد. عقد ما بعد الحرب كان ينُصّ على انسحاب، طُبِّقَ جزئياً وعلى مضض. في الجوهر لم يكن للانسحاب أي معنى لأن جهاز المخابرات تجذر بقوة في كل تفاصيل الحكم وفاض على كل المُعاملات والإجراءات المدنية منها والمُخالفة في حياتنا اليومية. معجزة إعادة الإعمار كانت عملية إثراء سريع للطبقة السياسية في البلد وحلفائهم في النظام السوري. هذه الخطط الغامضة لم تكن كُلّياً سرّية، تفاصيل كل خطة كانت غامضة وكنا نتلقى حكايات رسمية عن لماذا أسند هذا العقد إلى هذه الشركات بالتحديد ولماذا كانت مبالغ مرصودة لمشروع تضاعف فجأة ولماذا النظم المحاسبية كانت تفشل في مهماتها. ولماذا وزارات جديدة كانت تُنشأ. ولماذا كانت الميزانية العامة تُناقش في دمشق؟ وهكذا دواليك. الحكايات الرسمية كونت حبكة رسمية ولغة رسمية ومفردات وقواعد. فك الشفرات كان في أحيانٍ مسلياً وكان في أحيانٍ مُريباً. تعلمناه رغماً عنا بعفوية، مُنساقين لقانون الزمن الجبار.

بقدر ما كانت للحرب موسيقاها التصويرية المؤلفة من سيمفونية الانفجارات والأسلحة بقدر ما كان الما بعد الحرب له موسيقاه أيضاً، إنها سيمفونية ضجيج ورُشّات إعادة الإعمار (كانت فقط في النهار). عندما خطف صخب الحملة الدعائية العقول والقلوب، المستثمرون والمقاولون وباشاوات الحرب الجدد أطلقوا بحماس وتسرّع الإمكانيات والماكينات وجحافل العمال (غير الشرعيين) لاستعادة عز لبنان، على الأخص بيروت. وبالرغم من تغنّيهم بوطنيتهم المُدّعاه فإنهم كانوا ينتهزون فرصة الإثراء السريع. ورشات للإعمار كانت تثُبّت كل يوم في كل مكان، ولم يكن هناك أية رقابة عليا للتنظيم والتنسيق بعقلانية لهذه المبادرات الخاصة والدفاع عن الحق العام. التخطيط، المقاييس، الطابع المعماري، كل العوامل التي تدخل في خطة النمو المدروس والحفاظ على محيط سكني مقبول تم غض النظر عنها. قيل لنا إن بيروت ينبغي عليها أن تُسّارع خطاها كي تُعوض عن خساراتها الجسيمة، وإن التوقف عند هذه العوامل وأخذها في الاعتبار سوف يُعيق الحراك وكنا نتهم بتكدير الصفو العام.

أتذكر كيف كنت أصحو على الأصوات المدوّية لآلات البناء. حفارات صغيرة ذات أذرع طويلة تنتهي بأسنان حديدية تنبش في بطن بيروت الصخري، رتابة تكرار ضرباتها كانت توحي بالوحشية، الأسمنت الذي يتدفق بدون كل لم يكن يعد بالازدهار بقدر ما كان يعد بالضيق. لمن هذا التعمير؟ لم يكن مُهماً لمن، كان كورس الرسميين يقول لنا: "ابنوا وسيأتوا". وفي الحقيقة اتضح أن البناءات الجديدة والبرّاقة كانت تُبنى للأثرياء العرب الذين قُدّم لهم بيروت ولبنان على أنه موطنهم الثاني. أما البناءات متوسطة المستوى كانت تُبنى للبناني المهجر الذين حالفهم الحظ في مهجرهم. أما البناءات المتواضعة التي بنيت لنا نحن الناس العاديين ظهرت وانتشرت على أطراف بيروت في اتجاهاتها الأربعة. نحن أولاد البلد المقيمين فيها، الذين اختاروا البقاء. كنا مدعوين أن ننتقل إلى الضواحي الجديدة حيث الخدمات الأساسية من الماء والكهرباء والصرف الصحي لم تكن قد اكتملت بعد. هذه كانت حصتنا من معجزة التعافي.

بنود الاتفاق ضمن نص الدستور، ولكن الميثاق الوطني (الذي هو أساس البلاء) لم يُمس. خمسة عشر عاماً والحكمة من وراء هذا الاتفاق لم تُطبق بعد. في ظل عدم وجود رؤية للجمهورية المُسيَّرة على طريق الشفاء فإن الحيلة الأسهل بدت في التقهقر الفطري إلى صورة البلد فيما قبل اندلاع الحرب. أما نحن الناس العاديون فقد انسقنا وراء التحليق إلى هذا الماضي ولكن بالسرعة القصوى في اتجاه الحاضر. بعبارة أخرى فإنه لم يكن هناك أية خطة. فقط كان هناك حملة تسويقية مهولة لتشجيع الاستثمار في إعادة إعمار البلد وعلى الأخص بيروت. بعض المثقفين سجلوا سخطهم في الصحف وانتقدوا الحكومة على أنها أكثر حرصاً على تأهيل الحجر قبل البشر، حتى أصبحت مقولة: "الحجر قبل البشر" حدوتة عامة، سائقو التاكسيات، أصحاب الدكاكين، سياسيون طموحون، مناضلون.. صاروا يلوكونها.

على مدى السبعة عشر عاماً فإن علامات القذائف والرصاص والحرائق والقنص كانت قد تَجَنبت فقط قلة قليلة من البنايات. في الواقع فيما عدا بعض المنشآت العامة والأساسية مثل المطار والمرفأ والأنفاق والجسور والطرقات وبعض المؤسسات الأخرى فإن الحكومة لم تكن لديها أية نية في ترميم أي شيء، حتى ولا أي حجر. ولم تكن هناك أي نية في دعم الناس العاديين لترميم بيوتهم. كانت الحكومة تتحايل على خلق حراك يرتكز على خطة إعادة تأهيل وبناء وبناء قلب المدينة كما كانت قبل الحرب. أنشئت شركة عقارية خاصة مُعفاة من الضرائب ومُحصّنة ضد التدقيق ومنيعة ضد الجدال، كلّفت بتحديث البنية التحتية لوسط بيروت المُدمر والمحترق. وتم تأجير المساحات لمستثمرين عقاريين آخرين لإعمارها. أتذكر بوضوح المرة الأولى التي لاحظت فيها أول مبنى على الطراز التقليدي طالته يد الإصلاح أو بالأحرى الطلاء، كان يقع بالقرب من الخط الأخضر كما كان يُعرف أيام الحرب، ذلك الطريق الواسع الذي يتلوى كالثعبان قاسماً بيروت إلى قسمين مُتصارعين، كانت البناية تقع على إحدى مفارق هذا الطريق. إعادة الطلاء لم تكن جيدة وكانت خالية من الذوق، ولكنها كانت مُبهرة كأنها مُباهاة بالفعل الصائب.

كنا قد تعودنا على مناظر الواجهات المُشوهة والأبنية المُدمرة والجدران والأسقف المثقوبة، لم يكن لدينا أي وازع لأن نعمل سريعاً على ترميم ما كان يمكن ترميمه، منذ فترة طويلة لم تعد علامات الدمار والألم تزعجنا. كان هذا قدرنا وميراثنا من أيام الحرب. كانت هذه البناءات قد ابتدعت لنفسها جماليتها الخاصة. الكثير من الحبر سال على كونها أطلال حديثة أو أطلال الحداثة، والكثير من البروميد قد ذوّب لالتقاط شاعريتها أو استنباط معنى عميق بداخلها. السائحون والزوار المغامرون الذين جاؤوا في السنين الأولى لما بعد الحرب كانوا كثيراً ما ينفعلون. يتحمسون ويصورون ويوثقون بحماس. ونحن نقوم بدور الدليل السياحي لهم كنا نُسليهم بحكايات عن الصراع اليومي من أجل البقاء على قيد الحياة، لكي نُريح أرواحنا من عبء الشجن المدفون. النوع الآخر من السياحة في البلد كان سياحة الآثار، تلك الآثار التي تتميز بها مدن المتوسط ذات التاريخ البعيد والمُمتد إلى أيام الرومان والفينيقيين. هذه الأطلال الأثرية هي على النقيض، لأنها دلائل على أمجاد ماضية وليس على مأساة. المجد ليس أفقاً خصباً لاستلهام المجاز والكناية، باستثناء القومية المتعافية عن مسارها، ولكن هذه قصة مختلفة تماماً. أطلال حربنا التي تفوح منها الحداثة وخيبة ما بعدها، كانت أكثر إثارة وإلهام. البعض كان يراها كأنصاب، ذكرى رمزية لما فعلناه في أنفسنا وفي هذا البلد. والبعض الآخر يراها ذكرى لما فعله الآخرون بنا. والبعض اقترح أن يتم الاحتفاظ بعدد من هذه الأنصاب في حالاتها الخربة لردع أهل لبنان، ولردع الذين يُخَلخلون صواب أهل لبنان من الاستسلام لأبالسة الاقتتال. في العام 1993 كان عُمر الجمهورية بالكاد لا يتعدى الخمسين عاماً. وكانت قد شهدت ثلاثة صراعات على شكل حرب أهلية (شبه فرصتين وواحدة فعلاً طويلة). وشاعت فكرة الصراع الأهلي باعتباره جزء مُكوّنا لقدر الجمهورية. وأصبح شبح المأساة يهيم في أفق ما بعد الحرب. خفي ولكن ملموس، أحياناً يدنو بشؤمه ثم يبتعد جراء تدخل القوى العليا.

إنّ حراك إعادة الإعمار والتأهيل اشتعل بعد أن قامت الحكومة بحشد ضجيجها الإعلامي. تم طلاء واجهات المباني، البوابات الحديدية المُدَعمة للأبواب الخشبية إما تمت أزالتَها أو فقدت دورها الواقي بتركها مفتوحة ومفاتيح أقفالها نُسيت في قيعان الأدراج. الدكاكين صارت تَتُرك واجهاتها الزجاجية مكشوفة وأمست الأبواب المعدنية الجرّارة التي كانت تحميها من رصاصات الليل مطوية في مكانها العالي. أنوارها مُضاءة على الدوام. الشوارع التجارية صارت أقل قتامة وجزع في الليل، حتى أنها أصبحت لطيفة كَمَمْشَى. الأبنية التي كانت مُهترئة وباهتة الألوان دبّت فيها الحياة عندما طُليت بألوان الباستيل. سحر بيروت المتوسطي، المُضيء، الذي يدعو للاسترخاء ابتدأ في استعادة نفسه رويداً رويداً، الاحتفاءات الطويلة المُمتدة حتى غروب الشمس على موائد الوجبات استعادت نفسها رويداً رويداً. الترحال في الجغرافيا المُرتبكة لهذا البلد الصغير أصبح مثل الترحال في أفق مفتوح. الحواجز التي تَبَقَّت فقدت الكثير من قدرتها على السيطرة. عادت الهواتف تتواصل من جديد رويداً، كما أصبح مُمكناً الاتصال بأصدقاء قد ابتعدوا، تبادل أرقام الهواتف مع أناس جدد، إلغاء المواعيد، حجز تذاكر للمسرح، الاتصال بالمعشوق في ساعات متأخرة، مُطاردة أزواج خائنين... (كل هذا قبل انفجار موضة الهواتف الخليوية).

البعض الذي وُلِدَ خلال الحرب لم يكن يتخيل إمكانية حدوث مثل هذه الأشياء. كنا مُبْتَدئين في رغد العيش الذي كان يُسَوّق على أنه سبب وجود لبنان. الليالي الحمراء استعادت نفسها رويداً رويداً. في الحقيقة أنها لم تتوقف خلال الحرب ولكنها كانت مُختلفة، كانت مَدفُوعة بالحاجة إلى تحدي العنف فكانت مُلّونة بالسريالية والجنون. الليالي الحمراء فيما بعد الحرب لم يكن لديها مثل هذا الإيقاع. كانت ببساطة على شاكلة الليالي المُفتعلة والمُبتذلة في كل مدينة تعيش في صراع طبقي وتأخر في التنمية وادّعاء الكوزموبوليتانية في عصرنا هذا. فما بين الميثولوجيا التي ابتدعتها بيروت لنفسها على أنها عاصمة العرب للانحلال وللحياة المخملية وبين الاندفاع لابتكار مفهوم لرغد العيش فيما بعد الحرب صارت بيروت المقصد لإجازات أثرياء العرب الذين لديهم هذه الميول لارتكاب الآثام بدون احتشام.

كثيراً ما كُنتُ مُؤرّقة في سريري، مُستَمعة إلى صمت الليل في ساعات ما قبل الفجر. أترقب سماع صوت الرصاص والقذائف تنفجر بعيداً. لا شيء. أحياناً أسمع بدلاً عن ذلك أصوات المكابح المدوية للسيارات المُسرعة وصراخ السكارى العالي عند عودتهم إلى بيوتهم، وجامعي القمامة، بدون شك فإن ذلك هو أكثر الدلائل عقلانية على العودة للحياة الطبيعية. لم أكن مُعتادة على صفير عجلات السيارات أو على صراخ المحتفلين السكارى أو على جامعي القمامة. صمت البنادق كان مُربكاً. لم يكن لدي أي اشتياق للحرب ولكن كنت تائهة بسبب غياب معالمها. لسبب ما فإن شُحنات الخوف قد زالت من ذاكرتي وأصوات ضرب النار ظلت في ذاكرتي كأنها هي أصوات الليل.

استغرق الأمر سنتين أو أكثر كي يرحل عني هذا الشعور بالاغتراب عن الأشياء اليومية. المشي في الشوارع التي كانت مشهورة بأنها مرمى للقناصين، الذهاب للأحياء التي بعد الخط الفاصل والتي لم أكن أستطيع الذهاب إليها فيما قبل، شرودي في مناظر كأنني أراها لأول مرة.

خلال الحرب الأهلية. كان الموت مألوفاً في حياتنا اليومية. ولم تكن أمي من اللواتي يصررن على ارتداء السواد بشكل كامل، كانت تُفضل مزيجاً من الأبيض والأسود، أو الرمادي. ذكرياتي عن ذلك العزاء الأول ليست واضحة تماماً، أذكر أني ذهبت معها فحسب وخُضت تجربة هذا الطقس الاجتماعي لأول مرة. وبعد أن كثرت واجبات العزاء، أصبح هذا الطقس شائعاً في حياتنا الاجتماعية. في لبنان، الطقوس الاجتماعية المرتبطة بالموت تُركّز على العزاء أكثر مما تُركّز على الدفن. والعزاء يتبع الدفن، أما الجسد الميت فلا يُعرض على الناس الذين جاؤوا كي يقدموا التعازي لأهل الفقيد المكلومين. وعلى الرغم من عناوين الصحف التي كانت تسجل الموت كل يوم، كعملة للحرب الأهلية، ومع أني اعتدت على واجبات العزاء، غير أني لم أفهم أبداً ولو لمرةٍ واحدة المغزى الكامل من الموت.

إحدى أعز صديقاتي في أيام الدراسة مات والدها عندما كُنا في الرابعة عشر أو الخامسة عشر. مات بمُضاعفات عملية جراحية صعبة. لم يكن ضحية للحرب الأهلية بشكل مباشر، ولم يمت في ساحة القتال، لم يمت من رصاصة أو قذيفة. كان ضابطاً ذا رتبة عالية في قوى الأمن الداخلي، وكانت المهابة العسكرية تطغى على حنان طبعه، لذلك كنت دائماً أشعر تجاهه بالخشية والرهبة. وبعد مضي نحو أسبوع على يوم العزاء، كنت أستقلّ حافلة المدرسة في الصباح الباكر، وكان الطريق مزدحماً، وكنت شاردة أتأمل أولئك الذاهبين إلى أعمالهم، عندما رأيته مائلاً أمام عيني، مُرتدياً ملابس قديمة، رثة، يبيع الصحف والسجائر. بدا لي حقيقياً تماماً، وبالقدر ذاته الذي بدا فيه سائر الناس الآخرين حقيقيين. لم يكن شبحاً، كان يمد يده داخل السيارات عبر نوافذها ليحصل على النقود من الركاب. كنت مُقتنعة أنه هذا الرجل، وأنه لم يمت. ربما يكون قد ترك حياته التي كان يعيشها حتى لحظة موته المُفترضة ثم سعى إلى حياةٍ أخرى، لعلّه كان مُتعباً ولم يستطع أن يُتابع حياته كما كانت مع زوجته وبناته وابنه، والمنزل الجميل، والرتبة العسكرية. ولعلّه خطط لموتِه وقام بإخراج موته كي يتسنى له الهروب من حياته كما كانت. قد تكون تلك هي الطريقة التي ابتكرها كي يفلت من تلك دون أية مشاكل. الموت كان عُملة الحرب. وهذا كان يحدث لأناس كثيرين كل يوم. وكل شيء آخر، الطلاق، انكسارات العائلات، الفراق، كلها كانت تراجيديات غير طبيعية ومفجعة. فوجئت بنفسي أتقبل هذا السيناريو الذي رسمته للرجل دون تساؤلات كبيرة، حتى أني أحسست بالتضامن مع حزنه، وتقريباً تَفَهَّمْتُ عدم ارتياحِه لحياتِه التي كان مسجوناً فيها. ضمنياً وافقت على اختياره لحياةٍ جديدةٍ. حوّل الرجل موتهُ لمسرحيةٍ كان هو بطلها، وأصبح لديه الآن حياة جديدة، يعيش في مُجتمع آخر مع أناس آخرين يتصارعون من أجل العيش، يبيعون الصحف، العلكة، المناديل الورقية وأي شيء آخر. أناس يسيرون قُرابة الساعتين من مكان نومهم إلى أماكن أعمالهم، يستقلون الحافلة العامة. كان هذا هو قرار الرجل كي يكون سعيداً. هكذا ظَنَنْتُ، وظني مَلآني.. رويداً. رويداً. منذ تلك اللحظة، أخذت أرى بشراً أعلم أنهم رحلوا، أراهم يظهرون مرة أخرى وسط حيوات مختلفة تماماً. الموت لم يعُد نهاية الحياة، بل نهاية عيش مُحدّد، واختياراً واعياً لحياةٍ أخرى، لطريقة عيش جديدة.

كنت أعلم جيداً كيف يصل الإنسان إلى حدّ الإجهاد. كيف يحس بالاختناق، ويصل إلى شفير اليأس. لقد كان هذا مألوفاً بالنسبة لي. لذلك كان غالباً ما يحدث ذلك بالرحيل المفاجئ الذي لا عودة منه، فبين عشية وضحاها كان ثمة أناس يُعدون حقائبهم تاركين حيّهم، مدينتهم، ووطنهم، وإلى الأبد. وإلى جانب حضور العزاءات، اعتدت أيضاً على حفلات الوداع. وقتها كان يبدو الرحيل نهائياً، بنفس القدر الذي كانت معه: (إلى اللقاء) أو (نبقى نشوفك) نهائية. النظام البريدي كان مُنعدماً تماماً، وخطوط الهاتف تعمل على هواها فلم يكن هناك ثمة أمل في الحفاظ على أي اتصال مع أحد. حفلات الوداع كانت أكثر إيلاماً من العزاءات. أنا، نحن الذين بقينا مهجورين من الذين رحلوا، ألمُ قاسٍ أن تكون مهجوراً، ولم يكن هناك غير الوقت شفيعاً لنا من هذا الألم. تماماً مثلما يشفع لأحزان الموت. بعد فترة قصيرة اختلطت في ذهني حفلات الوداع بطقوس العزاءات، وأتذكر أني كنت أخشى أن أصبح من المهجورين.

لستُ متأكدة كيف انتهت الحرب، من المؤكد أن هناك تسلسلاً زمنياً- وهناك العديد في الواقع، وأنّ المؤرخين سيقترحون نظريات عديدة لنهاية الحرب. كانت هناك المعارك التي بدت حاسمة، وإن لم تكن نهائية، مفاوضات سرية في مدينة بعيدة بالسعودية، اتفاق لإنهاء الحرب، انتخابات نيابية مُسَرّعة، رئيس جديد للجمهورية، مجلس وزراء، مظاهرات عنيفة وإطارات تحترق عندما انهارت العملة الوطنية كُلياً، وأخيراً اغتيال مأساوي للرئيس الجديد. كل هذا على مدى عام واحد أو أقل. ربما هي بداية خاطئة ولكن لم تكن غريبة على تجربة الحرب الأهلية. مؤامرة؟ هذا دائماً جواب صحيح في لبنان. كان مُلفتاً أن المحاولة الثانية للبداية من جديد لم تتعثر باندلاع دورة أخرى من الاقتتال. كان الأمر يبدو كالحريق الذي يخمد جرّاء التغطية التي تحجب الهواء عنه. البعض قال إن هذه كانت علامة نهاية الحرب بمعنى أن الدولة استعادت السيطرة على الاقتصاد القومي. صار لدينا رئيس جديد للجمهورية ومجلس وزراء جديد، وفي هذه المحاولة الثانية أنقذت العملة الوطنية واستقرت فجأة. البعض قال إن هذه كانت علامة نهاية الحرب بمعنى أن الدولة استعادت السيطرة على الاقتصاد القومي، لكن هناك النظريات الأخرى التي تفترض أن الدولة تُثبت وجودها باحتكار مُمارسة العنف ولكنها نظريات لم تصح، لأن هذه السلطة كانت بيد النظام السوري المجاور. وكانت 12% من أرض الوطن، الطرف الجنوبي تحت الاحتلال الإسرائيلي حيث كانت تُطلق عليه اسم الشريط الحدودي الأمني. المُقاومة العسكرية كانت ناشطة هناك حتى سحبت الدولة الإسرائيلية جيشها ومراكزها والجهاز المحلي الحليف لها في العام 2000. ومن غير شك في أن ثمة أرشيفاً ومفاوضات دبلوماسية واتفاقات، لكن ليس في استطاعتي تحديد اللحظة التي استعدنا فيها عيشنا من حالة الحرب إلى حالة اللا حرب. لابد من أنّ التحول كان تدريجياً خطوة خطوة، لكن بالتأكيد كان ثمة صباح ما ابتدأ فيه أول يوم في الفصل الأول لما بعد الحرب. فلكل الروايات فصل أول، لحظةٌ ما يرسو فيها التطور الدرامي. أعرف أن هذا الصباح هو محض تفصيل صغير، لكن الفكرة هاهنا أننا قد تغيرنا، كأننا مُرغمون.. كأننا مدفوعون من داخلنا، تقمصنا أدواراً جديدة، ضحايا الحرب صاروا مواطني الجمهورية (المُعدّلة). شهود العيان البريئون صاروا مواطني الجمهورية. المُقاتلون، أعضاء الميليشيات، الأبطال واللا أبطال. كلنا وُلدنا من جديد. مواطنو ما بعد الحرب، أمراء الحرب صاروا أعضاءً بمجلس النواب ووزراء بالحكومة. لقد انتخبناهم مرة، مرتان، وثلاث مرات. عشرون عاماً، ولا زالت السلطة لديهم، وتم استبدال من اغتيل منهم بأبنائهم وبناتهم. التجمعات الأهلية والشبكة الاجتماعية للطائفية، تركيبة الخوف ورفض الآخر، شكلت المجتمع المدني للجمهورية. كان التحول مَهُولاً، كان ينطوي على أناس، أحياء، شوارع، وبنايات. أما الذين هاجروا إلى الأبد فقد عادوا في زيارات موسمية في فصل الصيف أحياناً، الذين ماتوا من الهجران. خوفي من الهجران تحول إلى ثكل، فهمتُ معنى الموت كلياً فيما بعد الحرب للمرة الأولى. فهمت قسوة النهاية التي يجلبها الموت.. النهاية التي لا عودة منها. فهمت الاشتياق الذي لن يتحقق إلى الأشياء التي أبداً لن تكون ثانيةً.

في أحسن الأحوال كانت التوجيهات غامضة بالنسبة لنا نحن المواطنون العاديون. الاتفاق السياسي الذي أفضى إلى إنهاء الحرب خرج بتعليمات واضحة للانتقال بالجمهورية إلى حالة السلم، كما أرسى ضمانات دستورية من أجل تفادي اندلاع حرب أخرى، وقد تم إلحاق

بيروتُ الثَكلى
بناءات مجفوّة.. وجغرافيا الاهتراء

تصوير فوتوغرافي: زياد عنتر

نص: رشا سلطي

وقفت عند مفترق الأوديون باريس، كان حاراً، وصاخباً. الزحام الذي يسبّبة الذهاب والإياب عند مفترق الطرق يجعل الشخص مَخفياً، بلا حراك، مُركِّزاً نظرة لمسافةٍ بعيدةٍ.. على ماضينا الذي هو أغرب من الموت، ولا أحد سوف يلحظ أن المرء يمكن أن يهمس بينة وبين نفسة، بهدوء، كما أفعل أنا الآن: سنبق طوال حياتنا أولاد الطلبعة مع اللفّحات الحمراء، دائماً ستبدو لنا الشمس لمّاعة كالقصدير، والسماء لها صدى الطبول، وليس يمكن أن نبرأ من ذلك، لا يمكن أن نتخطى الأفق الساطع الذي يبعد بضعة أيام من المشي. لماذا نكذب على أنفسنا. لن نكون أبداً كالآخرين الطبيعيين العاديين. مثل هذا الرجل الذي أراه يركب تلك السيارة الفارهة، حاشراً نفسه أمام عجلة القيادة بنفس الرقة التي ينحشر بها الكارت في ماكينة الصرّاف الآلي، فرش السيارة المُحَاك بعناية تامة يبتلعُهُ، ذراعه، رأسه. بكل أناقة يَدْلفُ إلى السيارة كما لو كان يرتمي بين أحضان العشيقة. مُبْتَسماً، مُرتَاحاً. يد واحدة على عجلة القيادة مُمْسكة بسيجار بني رفيع، البد الأخرى ممسكة بالهاتف، ليتصل برقم محفوظاً بذاكرتِه. سوف نقلّدهم.. سوف نُقلد هدوء سَريرتهم حين نقلدهم، سنسمح لفرش مُحاك بعناية أن يَبْتلعُنا ونحن نبتسم بنفس الراحة والهدوء. لكن في نهاية الأمر سنظل نحن البرابرة الصغار، الذين كانوا أصحاب الإيمان الأعمى بأن الأفق قريب، بضعة أيام من المشي، فقط سيظل هناك شرطاً وحيداً غير موجود فينا حين نقلدهم، وهو أن نعرف كيف نستمتع، هذه هي الدلالة التي ستكشف أمرنا.

هـذا المقطع من رواية "إعترافات حامل راية مهزوم"، أندريه ماكين

Building in Karantina

بناية في الكرنتينا

Khayyat Building, Wata al-Musaytbeh, built in 1983

بناية الخياط، وطى المصيطبة، بنيت عام 1983

هذا الكتاب هو طبعة جديدة من تعاون زياد عنتر ورشا سلطي "بيروت الثكلى: بناءات مجوفة.. وجغرافيا الاهتراء"، والذي تم إنتاجه وعرضه ونشره لأول مرة في بينالي الشارقة 9 عام 2009. بدأ مشروع "بيروت الثكلى" بلقاء بين عنتر وسلطي عام 2006، عندما اكتشفا أن كلاهما كانا يبحثان المباني المهجورة وعديمة الفائدة في لبنان التي شوهتها الحرب الأهلية اللبنانية. المشروع الذي يتألف من نص لسلطي وصور لعنتر، يكشف العلاقة بين العمارة الاجتماعية والعمارة المادية في لبنان ما بعد الحرب.

بينالي الشارقة 9 دعا الفنانّين للاستفادة من منصة البينالي للابتكار في مشاريع جديدة مثل "بيروت الثكلى: بناءات مجوفة.. وجغرافيا الاهتراء". وكان المشروع أيضاً المستفيد من أول برنامج إنتاج لمؤسسة الشارقة للفنون، وهي مبادرة تهدف إلى أن تكون داعماً رائداً لعمل الفنانين. ينبع نشر هذه الطبعة الجديدة لكتاب "بيروت الثكلى" من قبل مؤسسة الشارقة للفنون من مهمة المؤسسة لنشر الفن من المنطقة وكوسيلة لتحقيق مشاريع الفنانين.

مقدمة

بيروت الثكلى: بناءات مجفوة.. وجغرافيا الاهتراء

المؤلفون: زياد عنتر (صور)، رشا سلطي (نص)
المنسقون: شانون آيرز هولدن، أحمد مكية،
وسن يوسف
المحررون: إيتي بون مولر (لغة إنجليزية)،
إسماعيل الرفاعي (لغة عربية)
التصميم: كيمستري ديزاين
الاستشاريون: كارين مارتا وتود برادواي، KMEC

صدرت هذا المطبوعة لأول مرة عام 2009
من بينالي الشارقة

أعيد طباعته بمراجعات طفيفة عام 2021 من قبل
قسم التعليم والأبحاث، مؤسسة الشارقة للفنون

التوزيع من خلال الشراكة مع كتب KMEC عبر:

دستريبيوتد آرت ببلشرز (.D.A.P)
75 شارع برود، جناح 630
الولايات المتحدة الأمريكية - نيويورك ،
نيويورك 10004
Orders@dapinc.com

للتوزيع بالجملة والتجزئة والطلبات في الشرق الأوسط
ومنطقة الشرق الأوسط وشمال إفريقيا وأفغانستان
وباكستان:

مؤسسة الشارقة للفنون
الشويهين، منطقة الفنون
ص. ب. 19989، الشارقة
الإمارات العربية المتحدة
publications@sharjahart.org
sharjahart.org

صورة غلاف الطبعة الإنجليزية: فندق كوت دازور،
جناح، بُني عام 1973
صورة غلاف الطبعة العربية: برج المر،
وادي أبو جميل، بُني عام 1973
2021© مؤسسة الشارقة للفنون
حقوق النص 2021© رشا سلطي
حقوق الصور 2021© زياد عنتر

الترقيم الدولي (ISBN) 978-9948-02-483-5

طبع في دولة الإمارات العربية المتحدة

بيروتُ الثَكلى

بناءات مجفوّة.. وجغرافيا الاهتراء

تصوير فوتوغرافي: زياد عنتر
نص: رشا سلطي

SHARJAH ART FOUNDATION